SUPERCARS

MASERATI

Helen Lepp Friesen

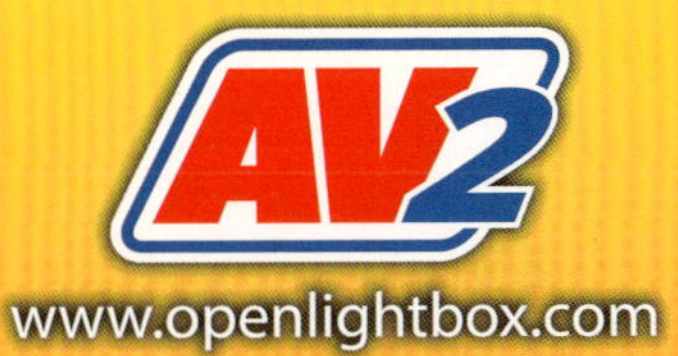

Step 1
Go to **www.openlightbox.com**

Step 2
Enter this unique code
BTPAKY49A

Step 3
Explore your interactive eBook!

AV2 is optimized for use on any device

Your interactive eBook comes with...

Contents
Browse a live contents page to easily navigate through resources

Audio
Listen to sections of the book read aloud

Videos
Watch informative video clips

Weblinks
Gain additional information for research

Slideshows
View images and caption

Try This!
Complete activities and hands-on experiments

Key Words
Study vocabulary, and complete a matching word activity

Quizzes
Test your knowledge

Share
Share titles within your Learning Management System (LMS) or Library Circulation System

Citation
Create bibliographical references following the Chicago Manual of Style

This title is part of our AV2 digital subscription

1-Year K–5 Subscription
ISBN 978-1-7911-3320-7

Access hundreds of AV2 titles with our digital subscription.
Sign up for a FREE trial at **www.openlightbox.com/tri**

SUPERCARS

MASERATI

CONTENTS

2 AV2 Book Code
4 Maserati Supercars
6 The Maserati Brothers
8 The Trident
10 Maserati through History
12 Famous Maseratis
14 At the Races
16 How It's Made
18 Today's Lineup
20 Tomorrow's Maserati
22 Maserati Quiz
23 Key Words/Index

MAS
MASERATI

RATI

MASERATI SUPERCARS

Supercars are rare and special sports cars. They are high-quality cars made with careful attention to detail. Only a limited number of supercars are created each year. They are very expensive because they are so rare.

Maserati is an Italian **luxury** car maker known for its excellent cars. With its unique vehicles, Maserati has been a leader in fashion. Every new Maserati design is admired and respected.

The **most expensive Maserati** sold for more than **$5.5 million** at an auction in **2013**.

THE MASERATI BROTHERS

The Maserati brothers, Alfieri, Ettore, and Ernesto, loved cars, engines, and racing. They turned their love of cars into a company. On December 1, 1914 in Bologna, Italy, they founded the Officine Alfieri Maserati.

During **World War I**, Alfieri and Ettore were called to fight, while Ernesto started making parts for aircraft engines. After the war, the company began to work on cars for other companies. The first car under the Maserati name, the Tipo 26, was released in 1926. It was a race car.

In 1937, the Maserati brothers sold their company to a businessman from Modena, Italy. The company was moved to this city in 1939.

Before founding the Officine Alfieri Maserati, Alfieri was a race car driver. After Alfieri died in 1932, another Maserati brother, Bindo, joined the company.

MAP OF ITALY

Maserati was founded in Italy, and its cars are still produced there. Maserati's headquarters remain in Modena.

World Map

Avvocato Giovanni Agnelli Plant, Grugliasco

Maserati Headquarters and Factory, Modena

Mediterranean Sea

SCALE 0 100 Kilometers 100 Miles

N S E W

LEGEND

- Key Location
- Italy
- Land
- Water

THE TRIDENT

In 1920, Maserati needed a logo. Alfieri, Ettore, and Ernesto asked their brother, Mario, to design the logo. Mario was a talented artist. The **trident** logo he created was inspired by Bologna's Fountain of Neptune.

The Fountain of Neptune is a well-known symbol of Bologna. It was made by the sculptor Giambologna in the 1560s.

MASERATI LOGO

The trident symbolizes strength.

Red and blue are the colors of Bologna's coat of arms.

MASERATI THROUGH HISTORY

The Maserati brothers established a renowned sports car company. Maserati cars are now recognized worldwide.

Italian race car driver Tazio Nuvolari drives the 6C 34 to win both the Modena and Naples Grand Prix.

1914

Officine Alfieri Maserati is founded in Bologna, Italy.

1934

1939

Maserati relocates from Bologna to Modena.

The first Maserati road car, the A6, is unveiled at the Geneva International Motor Show, in Switzerland.

1946

Maserati's **trimaran**, the Multi 70, breaks the record for sailing the Fastnet Original Course, a renowned sailing race. The Multi 70 completes the course in less than 24 hours.

2014

2021

Maserati reveals the Alfieri Concept Car.

FAMOUS MASERATIS

Some Maserati **models** have found their way to stardom on the big screen. Maserati cars are featured in three movies in the James Bond franchise: *Licence to Kill*, *Casino Royale*, and *No Time to Die*. A Maserati GranTurismo appears in the film *Limitless*, which stars Bradley Cooper and Robert De Niro. The movie *Percy Jackson & the Olympians: The Lightning Thief* shows a Maserati 4200 GT.

Licence to Kill, starring Timothy Dalton as James Bond, has an action scene with a Maserati Biturbo 425i.

Over time, Maserati has become a symbol of style, class, and status. Many celebrities have chosen Maserati cars. Singer Kylie Minogue drives a Maserati GranTurismo S. Music stars Katy Perry, Gwen Stefani, and Miley Cyrus are all Maserati fans. Soccer player David Beckham even became a Maserati brand ambassador in 2021.

Katy Perry has been seen driving a GranTurismo convertible, also known as GranCabrio.

Miley Cyrus's Maserati, a Quattroporte, was stolen in 2014.

In his first advertisement for Maserati, David Beckham drove a Levante Trofeo sport utility vehicle (SUV).

AT THE RACES

Maserati began as a race car company. Over time, its vehicles won many important racing events and took part in races from different motorsport categories.

Between 1950 and 1957, Maserati raced in **Formula 1 (F1)**. After this period, the company retired from racing. However, it kept on making race cars for other teams. Maserati returned to racing in 2004 with the MC12 model.

In recent years, Maserati decided to use its skill in creating **aerodynamic** designs to build a race boat. The Maserati Multi 70 has been taking part in offshore races since 2016.

Juan Manuel Fangio won the F1 World Championship with Maserati in 1957.

Maserati entered its first race, the Targa Florio, in 1926. Its Tipo 26 won the race in the 1,500 cc class.

In 1959, Maserati created a new type of chassis, or supporting frame, called the "Birdcage." It was used in sports cars.

The **Maserati Multi 70** is **70 feet** (21 meters) long and **55 feet** (17 m) wide.

Maserati had **70 F1 race starts** in the **1950s**.

The Maserati Multi 70 is led by skipper Giovanni Soldini.

HOW IT'S MADE

While some Maserati models are created in different plants, the main Maserati factory is still in Modena, Italy. The assembly line that is used to put together the mechanical parts has 12 stations. Cars stay at each station for about 25 minutes. At each stage, **engineers** inspect all the details to ensure the cars are reliable.

The Quattroporte and Ghibli models are made in a plant in Grugliasco, near Turin, Italy.

The Modena plant is still in the same location that Maserati moved to in 1939.

The **Grugliasco plant** can assemble up to **200** cars per day.

The **Modena plant** has more than **70 stations** in total.

The Modena plant is open to visitors. People can explore the history of Maserati and discover how the cars are produced.

The Grugliasco plant has about 1,300 employees.

TODAY'S LINEUP

Maserati models represent quality and prestige. The company offers different vehicles to meet the needs of its customers, including **sedans,** SUVs, and exciting sports cars.

Here are some of the Maseratis on the road today.

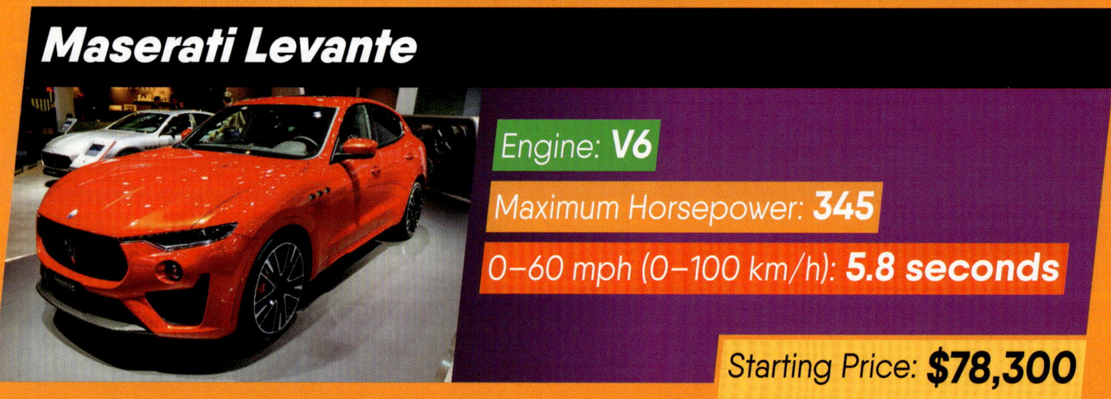

Maserati Ghibli S Q4

Engine: **V6**

Maximum Horsepower: **424**

0–60 mph (0–100 km/h): **4.7 seconds**

Starting Price: **$82,200**

Maserati Quattroporte S Q4

Engine: **V6**

Maximum Horsepower: **424**

0–60 mph (0–100 km/h): **4.8 seconds**

Starting Price: **$109,400**

Maserati Levante Trofeo

Engine: **V8**

Maximum Horsepower: **580**

0–60 mph (0–100 km/h): **3.8 seconds**

Starting Price: **$153,100**

TOMORROW'S MASERATI

Maserati has ambitious plans for the future. The company is working on several new models that will be launched by 2024. Some existing cars are getting a new look. Others will implement new technologies. For instance, the company plans to launch a **hybrid** version of the Ghibli car.

Maserati is also working on exciting brand-new models, such as the Grecale and the MC20. The MC20 is a two-seat supercar. Grecale is a compact SUV. Maserati plans to offer fully electric versions of these two models.

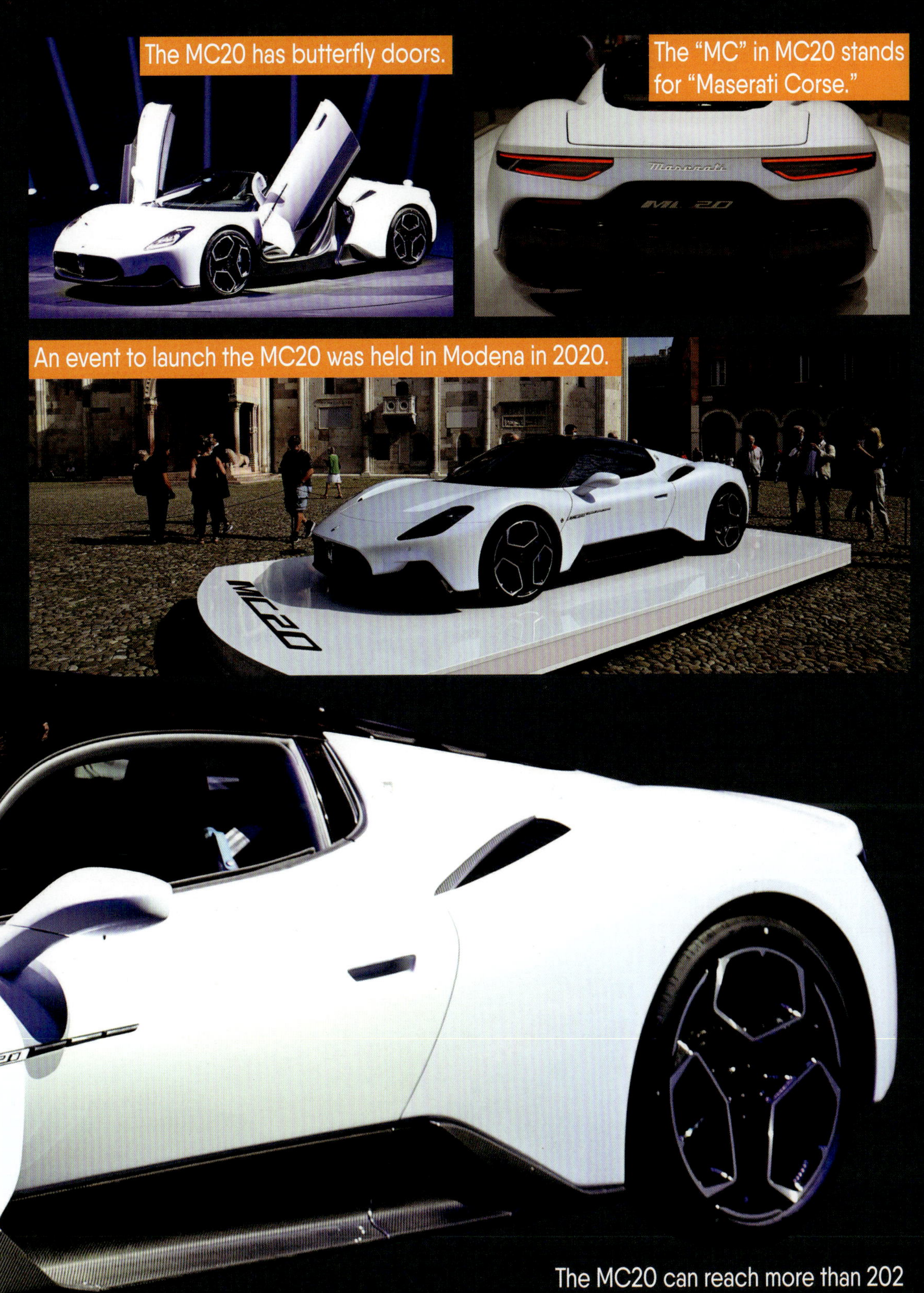

The MC20 has butterfly doors.

The "MC" in MC20 stands for "Maserati Corse."

An event to launch the MC20 was held in Modena in 2020.

The MC20 can reach more than 202 miles (325 kilometers) per hour.

MASERATI QUIZ

1 What does "MC" in MC20 stand for?

2 Where is the main Maserati factory?

3 Who started the Maserati company?

4 Who designed the Maserati logo?

5 Which Maserati models are made in Grugliasco?

6 How many people work at the Maserati factory in Grugliasco?

7 Who won the Formula 1 World Championship with Maserati in 1957?

8 What type of doors does the MC20 model have?

9 When did Maserati race in F1?

10 When did Maserati relocate from Bologna to Modena?

ANSWERS

1 "Maserati Corse" **2** Modena, Italy **3** Alfieri, Ettore, and Ernesto Maserati **4** Mario Maserati **5** Quattroporte and Ghibli **6** About 1,300 **7** Juan Manuel Fangio **8** Butterfly doors **9** Between 1950 and 1957 **10** In 1939

KEY WORDS

aerodynamic: something that reduces drag created by air

engineers: people trained to build things using different materials

Formula 1 (F1): the highest level of single-seat car racing

hybrid: a car that is powered by both a gas engine and an electric motor

luxury: the quality of being pleasing, comfortable, and expensive

models: the different car designs made by a company

sedans: cars that seat four or more people and have roofs that are fixed in place

trident: a three-pronged spear known as the weapon of Neptune, the Roman god of the sea

trimaran: a sailboat with three hulls

World War I: a war that was fought mainly in Europe from 1914 to 1918

INDEX

assembly line 16

Beckham, David 13
Bologna 6, 8, 9, 10, 22

engineers 16

Fangio, Juan Manuel 14, 22
Formula 1 (F1) 14, 15

Ghibli 16, 18, 19, 20, 22
Grecale 20

Levante 13, 18, 19

Maserati, Alfieri 6, 8
Maserati, Bindo 6
Maserati, Ernesto 6, 8, 22
Maserati, Ettore 6, 8, 22
Maserati, Mario 8, 22
MC20 20, 21, 22
Modena 6, 7, 10, 16, 17, 21, 22
Multi 70 11, 14, 15

Nuvolari, Tazio 10

Quattroporte 13, 16, 19, 22

trident 8, 9, 22

World War I 6

Get the best of both worlds.

AV2 bridges the gap between print and digital.

The expandable resources toolbar enables quick access to content including **videos**, **audio**, **activities**, **weblinks**, **slideshows**, **quizzes**, and **key words**.

Animated videos make static images come alive.

Resource icons on each page help readers to further **explore key concepts**.

Published by Lightbox Learning
276 5th Avenue, Suite 704 #917
New York, NY 10001
Website: www.openlightbox.com

Library of Congress Cataloging-in-Publication Data

Names: Friesen, Helen Lepp, 1961- author.
Title: Maserati / Helen Lepp Friesen.
Description: New York, NY : AV2, [2022] | Series: Supercars | Includes index. | Audience: Grades 2-3
Identifiers: LCCN 2021022179 (print) | LCCN 2021022180 (ebook) | ISBN 9781791138844 (library binding) | ISBN 9781791138851 (paperback) | ISBN 9781791138868 (ebook other)
Subjects: LCSH: Maserati automobile--Juvenile literature. | Sports car racing--Juvenile literature.
Classification: LCC TL215.M34 F75 2022 (print) | LCC TL215.M34 (ebook) | DDC 629.222/2--dc23
LC record available at https://lccn.loc.gov/2021022179
LC ebook record available at https://lccn.loc.gov/2021022180

Printed in Guangzhou, China
1 2 3 4 5 6 7 8 9 0 25 24 23 22 21

072021
101120

Art Director: Terry Paulhus
Project Coordinator: Sara Cucini

Photo Credits
Every reasonable effort has been made to trace ownership and to obtain permission to reprint copyright material. The publisher would be pleased to have any errors or omissions brought to its attention so that they may be corrected in subsequent printings. The publisher acknowledges Getty Images, Alamy, Wikimedia Commons, and Dreamstime as its primary image suppliers for this title.